Discovering ENGLISH CUSTOMS AND TRADITIONS

Margaret Gascoigne

Shire Publications Ltd

CONTENTS

ACKNOWLEDGMENTS

Very many people have been kind enough to answer enquiries concerning the customs mentioned in this book. Although too numerous to name individually, I must thank all the librarians, local authority officials, vicars, rectors and private enthusiasts concerned for so much help. Without their assistance the compilation of this volume would not have been possible.

Every effort has been made to ensure that the information given is correct, but customs have a habit of dying out and some of the dates are variable, so it is advisable to enquire locally before setting out to attend one of these functions.

Photographs are acknowledged as follows: Cadbury Lamb, plates 1, 4, 6, 8 and 12; Photocall Features, plate 2; Times Newspapers, plate 3; R. D. Barrett-Lennard, plates 5 and 7; G. Hodgson, plate 9; *Berkhamsted Gazette*, plate 10; Western Times Co. Ltd, plate 11; *Salisbury Times*, plate 13.

 First published 1969, reprinted 1971; second edition 1980, reprinted 1983. No. 66 in the Discovering series. ISBN 0 85263 506 0.

CUSTOMS AND THEIR ORIGINS

Our awareness of the past is as great today as it has ever been. Most of the customs recorded in this book have taken place for many years and still continue, forming a living link with history. It is impossible to convey the atmosphere of these events in words and their romance and excitement can only be fully appreciated by going to see for oneself.

Our forefathers were pagan before St. Augustine and the early Christians reached these islands and many of our customs originate in these far off times. Not all have pagan origins for some are memorials from feudal days, or of medieval charities and craft guild celebrations. Some are based on the whim of an eccentric who wished to perpetuate his memory in local society. Many customs, though widely separated geographically, have a common origin and some of these will be outlined here.

May Day celebrations

The festival of Flora, the goddess of fruit and flowers, was celebrated by the Romans at the end of April and beginning of May and all the traditional elements of our modern May Day festivities have their beginnings in these celebrations. Thus the flower-crowned May Queen personifies the goddess herself. The whole occasion was one of singing, dancing and general merriment. The houses were decorated with flowers, fruit and even whole trees; in addition every village or town had its festive tree standing in a central position, often stripped of its leaves and branches. Gradually it became customary to leave the same tree in position all the year round and decorate it afresh each May, and thus evolved the Maypole as we know it today. The dances that are performed round it were originally danced in honour of the god of fertility.

Rogationtide Blessings and Beating the Bounds

From very early times men marked and guarded their boundaries and invoked the gods to bless their domain and its products. At the festival of Terminalia the Romans used to honour Terminus—the god of boundaries—and at the festival of Ambarvalia in May they walked in procession through the fields and made sacrifices for the protection and growth of the newly sown crops. The early Christian church endorsed these ceremonies by the institution of the Rogation Days when men walked in procession to ask God's blessing on the fields and new crops, and at the same time walked the boundaries.

Many of these Rogation processions became very disorderly and were forbidden at the Reformation; but Elizabeth I granted permission for the clergy, church wardens and parishioners to walk in procession on Ascension Day to define the parish boundaries and stop at places en route to offer up prayers for good crops. The need for impressing the boundaries upon people in this fashion was very necessary when maps were few and the populace largely illiterate. As an aid to memory the boundary marks were beaten with willow wands, members of the party were bumped on the ground, or the boys present were themselves beaten.

In some localities these customs have survived over the years and in others have been fairly recently revived, while in coastal areas where fishing is the main industry, it is the waters that are now blessed.

Well Dressing

The decoration of their wells as a thanksgiving for the gift of pure water was another rite performed by our pagan ancestors. Well-dressing is a survival of this ancient well worship, for the early Christians, too, knew the value of their water supplies and adapted this ritual for their own purposes. So today the decoration and blessing of wells is observed as a Christian ceremony in various places, mainly in Derbyshire; in some it is an old and continuous tradition but in others a fairly recent revival or innovation.

The decoration of the well is an intricate task in which young as well as old participate, so perhaps the survival of this beautiful custom is ensured. The design usually depicts a religious theme and is executed by pressing flowers and petals into clay. Weeks of preliminary preparation are necessary, but the actual making of the picture has to be delayed until the last moment. The decorated well can usually be seen for a few days after the actual blessing, if the weather permits.

Blessing the Plough

The Christian church recognised four great agricultural festivals based upon the principal phases of farming:—ploughing and sowing, the season of young crops and rising corn at Rogationtide, the first fruits at Lammas in August and the final harvesting. The pagan custom of dragging ploughs through the streets and invoking the blessings of heathen gods upon them was taken over and it became customary to take a plough to church on Plough Monday (the Monday after the feast of Epiphany in January) for the blessing "God spede the plow". This ceremony would be attended by members of the Plow Guild—one of the great trade guilds of medieval times whose members were concerned with the tilling of the soil. This ancient custom is perpetuated in some places.

Clipping the Church

The ceremony known today as "Clipping the Church" also has pagan origins. The word "clipping" is used here in the context "embracing or enclosing"; the church is "embraced" by the people joining hands and encircling the building completely, showing the affection and regard felt for the Mother Church. This ceremony is thought to have its origins in the Roman feast of Lupercalia held to celebrate the god Lupercus, god of fertility and flocks. The rites included a sacred dance round the altar performed by young people and a sacrifice of young dogs. The people today encircle the church as the Romans encircled the altar, and at Painswick in Gloucestershire "Puppy Dog Pie" used to be on the menu in every household.

Rushbearing and Hay Strewing

It has been suggested that the strewing of hay on church floors, which still occurs annually in some places, may be connected with thanksgiving ceremonies which used to follow the hay harvest; but when churches had mud floors, rushes and hay were scattered for the utilitarian purpose of keeping the floor warm and dry. These would be renewed for the great feasts such as Easter, Whitsun and the church's patronal festival.

The heathen paganalia or village feasts were, once again, adapted by the early Christians and developed into the country Wake—the feast of the dedication of the church. At first this was observed on the actual saint's day, and later on the nearest Sunday, and of course for this feast the rushes were renewed. The occasion was one of general merry-making, with processions to the church, followed by dancing and sports. Undoubtedly there is a connection between the paganalia and the rather elaborate rushbearing ceremonies which still survive in the north; some of the intricate emblems known as "Rushbearings", which can be seen on these occasions, may be a survival from the medieval Mystery or Miracle plays.

Mystery Plays

The original Mystery or Miracle plays were medieval dramas in which the story and characters were taken from sacred history or the legends of the saints. Different scenes were allotted to the various craft guilds who performed them on mobile wheeled stages. The whole production was supervised by the town authorities. Four collections of English Miracle Plays survive and are named after the towns where they were performed; they are the York, Chester, Coventry and Wakefield (or Towneley) cycles.

Mummers' Plays

Mummers' plays are performed in various parts of the country at different times of the year; according to the season they are known by different names. Pace Egg Plays are performed at Easter, the Soulcakers act their drama near All Souls' Day in November and there are several Christmas mumming plays. They all, however, have the same central theme of death and resurrection and represent a relic of rituals performed by ancient peoples. The principal characters are St. (King, Prince, Sir) George, the Turkish Knight, the Doctor and Captain Slasher; various minor characters also appear, using different local names. After an introduction there is a duel and a death and the doctor brings the corpse to life again. These plays were transmitted orally for many generations and odd variations have crept in, but their common origin is obvious. It is only in recent times that the texts have been recorded.

Morris Dancing

Another survival from ancient times, which originated in rites connected with the fertility of the soil and the food supply, is Morris dancing. When the Christians arrived it became a form of communal entertainment, achieving great popularity in Tudor times. The numbers and costumes of the dancers vary considerably, but there are usually six or eight men in a "side", and they may be accompanied by such characters as the Hobby Horse, the Fool and Maid Marian.

Pace Egging

Eggs are traditionally associated with Easter, the egg being a symbol of continuing life and resurrection, and the custom of rolling brightly coloured eggs down a slope or hillside ("pace egging") is said to be symbolic of the rolling away of the stone from Christ's tomb. The word "Pace", a form of *pasch* or *paques*, derives from a Hebrew word meaning Passover. In pagan times eggs were a symbol of the Festival of Spring, the season of fertilisation and germination, and coloured eggs were exchanged by the Greeks, Romans, Persians and Chinese at their spring festivals, so this custom, too, may have a pagan origin.

Courts Leet and Baron

When law and order were maintained by the Lord of the Manor, before regular law courts were established, their functions were carried out by local manorial courts. Courts Baron dealt with purely manorial matters; Courts Leet dealt with all criminal offences and carried out all duties covered these days by County, Borough and district councils. They appointed various officials for this purpose. Most places which retain these courts do so for historical and traditional reasons, but a few still fulfil practical functions.

Quit Rents

A Quit Rent is a nominal rent paid by a tenant to the owner of land or property releasing the tenant from all other services to the owner. In former times the tenant was thus released from all feudal services. Many such rents have been paid for over seven hundred years and nowadays the people concerned often have no idea of the location of the property involved.

CUSTOMS OF THE COUNTIES

AVON

On the Tuesday after Easter the choirboys of St. Michael's **Bristol** partake of large buns known as "Tuppenny Starvers". This distribution, which has been made for over two hundred years, probably started as a treat for the choir in the days when poorer people ate only black bread.

Under a bequest dated 1493 the floor of St. Mary Redcliffe church is strewn with rushes on Whit Sunday, and a memorial sermon is preached at a special service attended by the Lord Mayor who goes in procession to the church accompanied by other civic officials; this commemorates a wealthy merchant of the city who restored the church in the fifteenth century and later became a priest.

The ruin of St. Anne's Well was acquired by the Corporation in 1924 and on or about July 25th annually the clergy and parishioners of St. Anne's church, Brislington, make a pilgrimage to this old shrine, reviving an old custom. An Indian pilgrimage is made annually on September 27th to the tomb of Rajah Ram-Mohun Roy in Arnos Grove Cemetery. He came to this country in 1831 as the representative of the King of Delhi and died in 1833.

The opening of the Pie Powder Court regulating local fairs takes place on September 30th and the annual Redcliffe Pipe Walk occurs in October. Permission granted in the twelfth century for the ministers of St. Mary Redcliffe to convey water from a well, known as Rugewell, via a conduit to the church, is commemorated when the Vicar and parishioners walk the course of the pipe.

The Mummers' Play performed annually on Boxing Day at **Marshfield** was revived in 1929. The players for this eight hundred year old play are attired in paper streamers.

BEDFORDSHIRE

At **Ickwell** May Day Festival, held for four centuries, children walk in procession to the village green for the crowning of the May Queen. There is a permanent Maypole round which some intricate and colourful dances are performed, traditional May Day songs are sung and two "moggies"—traditional characters in bizarre dress and with blackened faces—go round with collecting boxes.

BERKSHIRE

The **Aldermaston** Candle Auction, conducted by the vicar, takes place every third year on December 13th in the village hall at 8 p.m. It is for the triennial rent of a piece of land known as Church Acre. A horse-shoe nail or pin is placed one inch from the top of a tallow candle, the candle is lit and bidding commences. When the candle has burnt down as far as the nail, this drops out onto an adjacent tin plate, and the highest bid before this occurs secures the rent of the field for the next three years.

A muddy form of football unique to the College has been played annually at **Eton** on November 30th—St. Andrew's Day—since the eighteenth century. Known as the Wall Game, it is played between teams of Collegers, scholars who live in the old college, and Oppidans, the remaining majority of full fee paying boys who live in boarding houses outside the college precincts. Another form of football exclusive to the College, known as the Field Game, is played at Eton in the Michaelmas Term under rules made in 1847.

Hungerford is renowned for its Hocktide celebrations on the second Tuesday after Easter. The Town Crier, blowing a seventeenth century horn, summons members to a meeting of the Manorial Court in the Town Hall. Certain officials, including two Tutti-men, are elected. The Tutti-men, carrying long staves decorated with spring flowers and topped with an orange, accompanied by the Orange Scrambler who has a sack of oranges, visit the houses of all the commoners where they exact a penny toll from the men and a kiss from the women; oranges are given in exchange. After a civic luncheon a blacksmith performs the ceremony of "Shoeing the Colt"—driving a nail into the shoes of visitors and new commoners. Pennies and oranges are thrown to the children and there are various other events during the day. All this celebrates the granting of certain fishing rights to the town by John of Gaunt in the fourteenth century. The manor of Hungerford was originally owned by the Crown and was given to John of Gaunt, the founder of the House of Lancaster, in 1366. Any monarch passing through the town is presented with a red rose, the Lancastrian emblem; the present Queen received one in 1952.

The oldest surviving charity to be decided by casting lots takes place in **Reading** on the Thursday after Easter in St. Mary's Church House. Three girls, all of whom have served faithfully and well in one Reading household for at least five years, draw lots for twenty nobles, left by John Blagrave in 1611.

The **Ufton** Bread Dole, which has been distributed over four hundred times so far, is still dispensed annually at Ufton Court on a date near the middle of Lent. Bread is distributed to the residents of the parish and sheets to those on an agricultural wage.

At St. George's Chapel, **Windsor** Castle, in June the Sovereign attends a service for the Most Noble Order of the Garter. There is a procession of the Knights of the Order in their magnificent robes.

BUCKINGHAMSHIRE

Ever since Lady Lee's death in 1584 a fresh red flower has been kept on her memorial in the vestry of **Aylesbury** parish church. The inscription on her monument, which depicts her with her three children, requests "Goode frend, stick not to strew with crimson floures, This marble tombe wherin her cinders rest" and it is to be hoped this wish continues to be granted for the next four hundred years.

Another saint's day is celebrated in curious fashion every year at **Fenny Stratford** where St. Martin's Day (November 11th) is marked by the firing of the Fenny Poppers. The poppers, metal pots each weighing about twenty pounds, are taken from the belfry of St. Martin's church where they are normally kept, to a local sports ground. They are loaded with gunpowder and fired at 4-hour intervals from 8 a.m. This custom has been observed since the church was built in 1730.

The most famous of all pancake races takes place at **Olney** on Shrove Tuesday and this has become an international event; it is said to date from 1445, though it has by no means a continual record. It is a race for females over sixteen who have lived in the parish of Olney for at least three months. An apron and head covering must be worn. The course is 415 yards long and the pancake must be tossed at least three times in the course of the race. The winner receives a kiss from the ringer of the Pancake Bell and a prayer book from the Vicar.

Grass is strewn between the pews and along the aisles of the parish church of St. Peter and St. Paul at **Wingrave** on the Sunday nearest to St. Peter's day (the last in June or first in July). This is known locally as "Feast Sunday" and the ceremony used to be associated with a large fair on the village green, now no longer held.

CAMBRIDGESHIRE

When Dr. Wilde died at **St. Ives** he left provision in his will, dated 10th August 1675, for the income from £50 to be spent each year on bibles, which were to be given to six children of each sex who were of "good report, under twelve years of age and able to read the Bible". The bibles were to be allocated by casting dice! This ceremony is still observed on Whit Tuesday at noon.

On the Sunday after July 12th or this date if it is a Sunday the church at **Old Weston** is strewn with hay.

CHESHIRE

A soul-caking play is performed annually at the beginning of November in the village of **Antrobus.**

The **Chester** Mystery plays were revived in 1951 and are produced as a feature of the Chester Festival of Arts. They are one of the earliest surviving cycles of Mystery plays and were first performed in the early fourteenth century.

The Royal May Day Festival at **Knutsford,** usually held the first Saturday in May, is the only May Day celebration in the country entitled to use the prefix Royal, for in 1887 it was attended by the Prince and Princess of Wales. Another unique feature of this event is the decoration of the pavements with beautiful patterns and mottoes traced in coloured sand. This is a relic of a once common custom. There is a splendid procession followed by the crowning of the May Queen and a display of Maypole, Morris and country dancing. Maypole dancing may also be seen at **Lymm.**

The annual Rushbearing Service at **Macclesfield Forest** church (Forest Chapel), the only service of its kind in Cheshire, takes place on the second Sunday in August. Locally-gathered rushes are placed on the church floor and left for a week. The service is normal Evensong but a special Rushbearing hymn, composed at the beginning of the century by a former vicar, is sung and the sermon is preached in the churchyard.

Neston Ladies' Walking Day, usually the first Thursday in June, has been an annual event since the club was founded in 1814 as a female friendly society. Members carrying white staves topped with flowers walk in procession to the church for a service, then to the Market Cross for a hymn, prayer and blessing and finally to a nearby hall for tea.

One Friday in early July is Walking Day in **Warrington**. Children from churches of all denominations take part, the town centre is closed to traffic and shops are shut as about ten thousand children, watched by about forty thousand people, walk through the town. This event was started in about 1833 by the Rector who saw the neglect and poverty suffered by the children as a result of the nearby Newton races held annually at this time. He persisted in organising this walk every year against much opposition and now the races are no longer held but Walking Day survives.

CORNWALL

The lighting of Midsummer Bonfires, an old pagan custom performed at the time of the summer solstice and adapted by early Christians to honour St. John, was revived by the Federation of Old Cornwall Societies after the First World War, and takes place on St. John's Eve—June 23rd. A chain of bonfires is lit across Cornwall soon after sunset; the fires are blessed and wild flowers and herbs are burnt; the blessing is spoken in the Cornish language. In some places couples jump through the flames to ensure good luck.

The Blessing of the Mead used to take place at **Gulval** on August 24th—the feast day of St. Bartholomew, the patron saint of bee keepers and honey makers.

Helston's May Day celebrations, better known as the Furry Dance, take place on May 8th (the feast of the Apparition of St. Michael) or the nearest Saturday. The streets are decorated and various dances are performed throughout the day, commencing at 7 a.m. The principal dance at noon is led by the Mayor and the last dance, in which everyone joins, begins at 5 p.m.

The ancient **Marhamchurch** Revel, held on the Monday after August 12th (the feast of St. Marwenne), commemorates the saint who brought Christianity to the village. The Queen of the Revel, elected from the village schoolchildren, is crowned by Father Time on the spot where the saint's cell stood. A procession round the village ends at the Revel ground where there is country dancing, Cornish wrestling and amusements for all.

The 'Obby 'Oss celebrations at **Padstow** take place on May Day itself. The fun begins at midnight on April 30th, when the Morning Song is sung outside the Golden Lion Inn and a procession moves through the decorated town singing outside each house. Later in the day the grotesque "Hobby Horse" appears accompanied by the Teaser, other oddly dressed characters and a band. The Hobby Horse dances through the streets during the day, "dying" at intervals until he is finally laid to rest late in the evening. Some say the Hobby Horse recalls an occasion in the fourteenth century when French raiders were frightened off by a hobby horse at the harbour entrance, and over the years this has become entangled with traditional May rites; but the explanation of the origin of this strange creature may not be quite so simple.

Hurling the Silver Ball at **St. Columb Major** occurs on Shrove Tuesday and the following Saturday week. The ball is made of wood encased in silver and the goals are over a mile apart. The game can best be described as a violent form of rugby in which "Town" plays "Country"; there may be up to one thousand in each team and if the object of the game —to score a goal—is not accomplished, then placing the ball beyond the parish boundary achieves victory.

A similar game is played at **St. Ives,** traditionally on Feast Monday (the Monday of Candlemas week in February), but possibly the following Monday. The game commences at 10.30 a.m. when the Mayor throws the ball from the wall of the parish church. The ball is passed from person to person as the game proceeds and whoever holds it at noon is declared the winner and receives a small prize from the Mayor in return for the ball.

Every fifth year St. Ives is also the scene of a curious ceremony which commemorates the death of a local benefactor—John Knill. It takes place on St. James's Day, July 25th, and should next occur in 1981. Knill built a monument to himself on Worvas Hill, just outside the town, and left provision for ten small girls clad in white to dance round it to the tune of the Old Hundredth Psalm played on a violin, the children and musician being suitably rewarded. This has become a civic ceremony with the Mayor leading a procession to the monument.

CUMBRIA

Ambleside Rushbearing used to take place on the Saturday nearest St. Anne's Day (July 26th), but more recently has been held on the first Saturday of the month near the Feast of the Visitation of St. Mary (July 2nd), to whom the church is dedicated. A procession of children and others carrying their "bearings" (crosses made of rushes, wooden frames of various shapes decorated with flowers and rushes, or baskets of flowers) walks through the streets to the Market Place, where the Rushbearers' Hymn is sung. This is followed by a church service, after which gingerbread is distributed to all who take part.

There was a long and active tradition of the Mumming Act in the **Barrow-in-Furness** area up to the 1920s. The Players were known locally as the Pace Eggers and each village had its own particular version. Many of these have been collected and a representative text has been compiled. This is now performed regularly in a number of places in the area on Easter Monday and the previous Saturday by some of the Furness Morris Men.

Rushbearing at **Grasmere** occurs on the Saturday nearest St. Oswald's Day—August 5th. A procession led by the clergy, followed by girls carrying a sheet full of rushes and by villagers each with their rushbearing of traditional design, walks through the village. A special hymn is sung and at the church, where the procession ends, rushes are arranged on the floor before a special service; again gingerbread is distributed afterwards. The famous Grasmere sports, which have over one hundred years continuity, are held on the Thursday nearest to August 20th.

The first Saturday in July is the date for the Rushbearing at **Musgrave,** where there is a procession through the village to the church, a service, tea for the children and sports.

The old custom of tying churchyard gates at weddings occurs in parts of the county, and Pace Egging still takes place at **Penrith** on Easter Monday.

Though the church at **Warcop** is dedicated to St. Columba, the Rushbearing is held on St. Peter's Day—June 29th, and locally it is known as Peter Day rather than Rushbearing. The procession, headed by a band and banners, walks through the village along to the church. The girls carry or wear crowns of flowers built on wooden or wire frames; boys carry crosses made of rushes. In the church these are placed on the floor round the altar where they remain over the following Sunday; then they are hung at the back of the church until a few days before the next Peter Day. After the service there is tea followed by sports.

There is a lively street game of football played in **Workington** on Good Friday, Easter Tuesday and the Saturday following, between teams known as Uppies and Downies.

DERBYSHIRE

Of all the traditions and customs still observed in this county well-dressing is undoubtedly the most famous, and rightly so for the "dressed" wells are a most beautiful sight.

The five wells at **Tissington** are dressed at Ascensiontide. June well-dressings include **Wirksworth, Ashford in the Water, Youlgrave, Tideswell** and, at the end of the month, **Hope.** In July this event takes place at **Buxton** and **Marsh Lane near Eckington.** August sees well-dressings at **Bonsall, Stoney Middleton, Bradwell, Barlow, Eyam** and right at the end of the month **Wormhill,** where the event carries over into the beginning of September. Exact dates may be obtained from the Peak Park Information Centre, Bakewell.

The lead mining industry in the Peak District is controlled by the Barmote Courts. These courts, which are the oldest industrial courts still extant in England, have powers to deal with all disputes concerning lead mining and ownership of mines; they record the ore obtained, for payment of dues and tithes. The **Wirksworth** Barmote Court meets in April and October and the **Eyam** Court usually meets the previous day.

A religious event which has been held for at least three hundred years takes place on the first Sunday in July near Ladybower Reservoir. This is the **Alport Castle** Woodlands Love Feast. At a time when Nonconformists were heavily penalised they met in this lonely place to hold services and the Methodists have met here ever since. There is a service in the morning and at the Love Feast in the afternoon worshippers testify what religion means to them, and receive a small piece of cake and a sip of water from the loving cup.

The famous **Ashbourne** Shrove Tuesday Football is still played. Two teams compete, the Up'ards—those born to the north of the Henmore stream which divides the town, and the Down'ards—those born to the south of the stream. The goals are set three miles apart and play can go on until after midnight if a goal is not scored earlier.

Towards the end of July the ceremony of "Clipping the Church" is observed at **Burbage,** near Buxton.

At **Castleton** on May 29th (Oak Apple Day) the escape of Charles II from the Roundheads is commemorated with a procession in the evening. The "King" and the "Queen", both on horseback, lead the way. Part of the King's costume consists of a huge garland made of flowers and foliage which almost envelops him. This is removed when the procession reaches the churchyard, and placed on top of the church tower where it remains for about a week. It appears that these celebrations for the King became associated with older May Day rites at some time.

On the last Sunday in August a Plague Commemoration Service which is held at **Eyam** in the Dell, recalls the action of the villagers who, when the Plague struck the village in 1665-66, isolated themselves from the outside world at the instigation of the Rector, and prevented the spread of the disease to the surrounding district.

The Shrove Tuesday Pancake Races at **Winster** have been run since at least 1870.

DEVON

At **Ashburton** officials appointed at the meetings of the local Courts Leet and Baron in November tour the town sometime in July for the annual Ale Tasting ceremonies. The Portreeve, Ale Tasters and others visit the inns to taste the ale and if it is satisfactory the landlord receives a sprig of evergreen to put over his door. Bread Weighing ceremonies are also held.

Andrew's Dole is still distributed annually on January 1st to the poor and aged in **Bideford;** John Andrew, who died in 1605, left a plot of land the rent from which was to be used for this purpose. This money is augmented from the Mayor's Christmas Appeal Fund and a loaf of bread and ½lb. butter is given to anyone over sixty. The Manor Court, which commenced in the 1880's when the Manor was conveyed to the aldermen and burgesses of the borough, meets once a year on the Saturday after Easter to hear suggestions from local people for improving the town and to appoint the People's Churchwarden. The Beat the Clock Race, in which competitors tried to race across the bridge while the clock struck eight, no longer takes place since the clock stopped and the bridge was closed for repairs; instead there are junior and senior Around the Town races on the eve of the Regatta.

The **Exeter** Plough Sunday Service (on the first Sunday after January 6th) is held in the Cathedral in conjunction with the Young Farmers. A plough is drawn from the great west door to the space before the Golden Gates where it is blessed.

The old custom of "tip-toeing" is still observed at **Gittisham.** On Shrove Tuesday children go to all the houses in the area chanting "Tip tip toe, please for a penny then we will go". They divide the money received between them.

The annual conker contest held on the Wednesday nearest October 20th at the New Inn, **Goodleigh,** near Barnstaple, is played with locally collected conkers and often over one hundred contestants participate. At **Ipplepen** Beating the Bounds takes place at irregular and infrequent intervals. The last two beatings were in 1910 and 1950. A member of the party making the ten hour hike is bumped on the boundary stones. One of the attractions at the village show held on the third Saturday in July is Maypole dancing and the ancient distribution of the Feo Fee money still takes place annually at Christmas.

On Good Friday at **Ideford** the Borrington Dole is distributed. The Rector and churchwardens stand at one end of the tomb of Bartholomew Borrington and lay twenty shillings on its flat top. The beneficiaries come one by one to the opposite end and pick up their money.

Maypole dancing takes place at **Kingsteignton** on Spring Bank Holiday Monday. It also occurs down at **Lustleigh** on the first Saturday in May. Here is takes place in a large orchard — Town Orchard — in the centre of the village and a few years ago this was bequeathed to the parish to be used as a May Day site for ever.

At **Ottery St. Mary** on November 5th young men amuse themselves carrying burning tar barrels about the village.

The giant **Paignton** Pudding is made to celebrate special events and portions are available for all comers. The institution of the new Borough of Torbay in 1968 was such an occasion.

The curiously named Fyshinge Feast, held annually at **Plymouth** on a convenient date in June or July, commemorates the bringing of water to the town in 1590 from the river Meavy by Sir Francis Drake and the annual "Survey of the Works and the Head Weir" which used to be very necessary to ensure that the tinners were not diverting the town's water supply for their own uses. The Council and guests meet on the lawn by the Head Weir and toast the memory of Drake in river water, and his descendants in mulled ale that they may "never want wine". Luncheon, including grilled trout from the Burrator Reservoir, is served at the head of the lake.

The Turning of the Devil's Boulder, when a large rock lying under an ancient oak tree in the square at **Shebbear** is turned over with great ceremony every November 5th, is said to be one of the oldest annual customs in the country; if this stone, allegedly dropped by the Devil, is not turned once a year ill luck will befall the village.

DORSET

May 13th (12th if 13th is a Sunday) is Garland Day at **Abbotsbury.** The children carry garlands of flowers they have made round the village and finally place them on the War Memorial. The garlands are elaborate structures of traditional shape, mounted on frames and carried on poles; when there were fishing boats in the village they were taken out to sea and thrown into the water, originally as a pagan sacrifice to the sea.

At **Mudeford**, near Christchurch, the annual Blessing of the Waters takes place from a boat offshore.

For over three hundred years the Court of Purbeck Marblers has met on Shrove Tuesday at **Corfe Castle** for the election of officers and the initiation of apprentices. These boys each have to convey a quart of beer from the Fox Inn to the Town Hall where the Court is held, while the Marblers try to upset it. If it reaches its goal intact the apprentice becomes a freeman of the court on payment of a fee. After the meeting, in order to preserve an ancient right of way to Ower Quay from which the marble used to be shipped, a football is kicked along the old road.

The Perambulation of the Bounds of the **Island and Royal Manor of Portland** takes place every seventh year and is next due in 1981. The Court Leet of the Royal Manor does this on Ascension Day; at their annual meeting in November they are concerned mainly with the Commoners' rights and the common land of the island.

The distribution of Christmas Pennies at **Sherborne** castle, which apparently originated in the eighteenth century, is still made on Christmas morning.

On the third Sunday in July the procession to commemorate the **Tolpuddle** Martyrs, organised by the National Union of Agricultural Workers, takes place. Six agricultural labourers of the village organised themselves into the first Trade Union in 1834; this was regarded as a conspiracy in restraint of trade, and they were transported to Australia. After widespread agitation they were later granted a free pardon.

DURHAM

In **Durham** curfew is rung every night at nine o'clock, except on Saturdays, for there is a legend of a man who went alone to ring the bell one Saturday evening and who disappeared never to be seen again. The singing of anthems from the Cathedral tower on May 29th is in honour of the restoration of Charles II; originally it took place on October 17th to commemorate the victory of the Battle of Neville's Cross in 1346, when Queen Philippa in the absence of her husband Edward III in France, repelled a Scottish invasion. The monks' contribution to the battle was the singing of Mass from the tower for an English victory and the promise of a special annual Mass if the Queen was victorious.

The Durham Miners' Gala, which takes place on the third Saturday in July, started in 1871. For this, "the greatest trade union demonstration in the free world", the city centre is closed to traffic as the various miners' lodges march in from the outskirts carrying banners and accompanied by bands; they assemble on the riverside race course where amusements are provided for all tastes. A Miners' Festival Service is held in the Cathedral.

Sedgefield on Shrove Tuesday is the scene of a Shrovetide football match. The goals, a stream and a pond, are situated five hundred yards apart. The game commences at one o'clock when the verger throws a specially made ball into the air. A general melée ensues, and the game finishes as soon as a goal has been scored.

EAST SUSSEX

Good Friday skipping, a once common custom in Sussex and believed to make the crops grow, now survives only at the Rose Cottage Inn, **Alciston** where people skip on Good Friday morning using a long rope provided by the landlord. At nearby Brighton this day was known as "Long Rope Day" until about 1850, an acknowledgment of the practising of this custom by the fisherfolk on the beach. On the same day an old-established marbles match takes place at **Battle** against nearby Netherfield and there is a distribution of hot cross buns. There is a Pancake Race at **Bodiam** on Shrove Tuesday.

At **Hastings** daily at 6.30 a.m. there is a "Dutch Auction" in the Fish Market; the auctioneer names a higher price than he expects to obtain for the day's catch and gradually reduces it. The first person to make a bid gets the fish. On the Wednesday before Ascension Day (sometime in May) the Rectors of All Saints and St. Clement's churches conduct a service on the foreshore at which the Blessing of the Sea takes place. The procession leaves the church at 7 p.m. Since 1897 an annual pilgrimage has been made from the church of St. Mary Star-of-the-sea to the ruins of the Chapel of Our Lady in the castle for the celebration of Mass; this usually occurs on the last Sunday in July. The title of Champion Town Crier of England is awarded after an annual contest which takes place in the town in August. All contestants, many of whom wear magnificent uniforms, read the same 150-word text, following the customary cries of "Oyez, Oyez".

November 5th at **Lewes** is celebrated with torchlight processions, burning of effigies, firework displays and rolling of lighted tar barrels down the street. This commemorates the martyrdom of seventeen local people burned at the stake in the reign of Mary Tudor, as well as Guy Fawkes. The events are organised by several Bonfire Societies.

Little Edith's Treat takes place each year at **Piddinghoe** on July 19th. Edith Croft died in 1868, aged three months and to commemorate the baby her grandmother made an endowment of £100 to be expended on the baby's birthday. There is a church service followed by children's races and tea.

Rye's Guy Fawkes celebrations include the burning of a boat on the Saltings, recalling the burning of captured boats by the townspeople when the French used to raid the town. Here, on Mayoring Day, towards the end of May, the Mayor and other council officials throw hot pennies from the Town Hall windows at noon to children in the street.

ESSEX

The opening of **Colchester's** Oyster Fishery takes place on a variable date in September. The Mayor, Town Clerk and Mace Bearer in their ceremonial dress, travel to Brightlingsea with members of the council. From here they go by boat to Pyefleet Creek, where oysters are fattened, and an Ancient Proclamation is read declaring the Fishery open for the season. All present partake of gin and gingerbread, the Loyal Toast is drunk, and the Mayor makes the first dredge of the season. Towards the end of October (about 20th) the Oyster Feast takes place. This was already an old custom at the time of Charles II, connected with the opening of St. Denys' Fair.

The ceremony of the **Dunmow** Flitch Trials, held to reward couples who managed to live in matrimonial happiness for at least a year and a day, dates from at least 1104. The event has a chequered history, but since 1949 several trials have been held. A mock court presided over by a judge, with a jury of six spinsters and six bachelors from Dunmow parish, conducts the trial of claimants.

Sailing barge races have been held at **Southend** for over one hundred years, usually in June; there are only thirty six of these vessels still in full commission. The annual Whitebait Festival in September originated in the early eighteenth century and was revived in 1934. A service for the Blessing of the Catch, attended by the Mayor, takes place in the morning off the pier and the catch is served at a dinner in the evening.

Thaxted is a noted Morris dancing centre. Dancers tour the locality at Easter and Whitsun and there is a festival in June.

GLOUCESTERSHIRE

When Queen Matilda fell in love with the Lord of the Manor at **Avening** and was rejected, she had him put in prison, where he died. Regretting her action, she caused the church to be built, attended its consecration in 1080 and gave a great feast afterwards at which wild boar was served. Nowadays after evensong in the church on the Sunday following Holy Cross Day (September 14th), pig-face sandwiches are served in a suitably transformed village hall, recalling the feast. On Pig Face Day, as it is known locally, these sandwiches may also be obtained at the local inns.

Cooper's Hill near **Birdlip** is the venue for a cheese rolling contest on Spring Bank Holiday Monday. This is a survival of the five hundred year old ceremony which preserves the grazing rights of the villagers of Brockworth-on-the-Hill. A large cheese is rolled down the hill chased by the contestants, and the winner keeps the cheese and receives a small money prize.

At **Bisley** on Ascension Day there is a well dressing. On Summer Bank Holiday Monday **Bourton-on-the-Water** is the scene of a five-a-side game of water football played in the river Windrush. This game was first played to celebrate the coronation of Edward VII.

The Verderer's Court of Attachment of the Forest of Dean meets regularly in the Speech House at **Coleford;** many of its duties have been curtailed, and it now deals mainly with matters arising out of encroachment of Crown lands.

"Clipping the Church" at Painswick takes place on the Sunday nearest September 19th. The children, choir and clergy of the parish church and daughter churches walk in procession round the churchyard; finally they join hands encircling the church completely, while a special "Clipping" hymn is sung. Buns are then distributed to the children in place of the traditional Dog Pie.

St. Briavels claims the distinction of being the home of the oldest unbroken custom in the county. On Whit Sunday after evening service the vicar and churchwardens throw small cubes of bread and cheese from a platform on the church wall to people assembled for the ceremony. This seven hundred year old event retains for the village the right to gather firewood in Hudnalls wood.

HAMPSHIRE

A once common custom was the hanging of a Maiden's Garland—usually a paper crown decorated with rosettes—in church on the death of a young bachelor or spinster of good character. Old garlands may still be seen in some churches but at **Abbotts Ann** the custom is still maintained.

The villagers of **Cheriton** and nearby **Tichborne** receive flour every Lady Day—March 25th—under an eight hundred year old bequest. The famous Tichborne Dole originated at the death bed of Lady Mabella Tichborne when she requested her husband to bequeath some land for an annual distribution of bread to the poor. He consented to give as much land as she could walk round carrying a burning faggot before this became extinguished. She managed to crawl round an area of over twenty acres and the land, still known as the Crawls, was set aside for this purpose and the distribution has been made ever since.

The Mumming play at **Crookham,** which has been performed for at least a century and probably much longer, may be seen annually on Boxing Day. Many of the players are dressed in paper strips, but Father Christmas wears traditional red and the Doctor a top hat and frock coat.

Lyndhurst Verderers' Court meets in the Verderers' Hall in the Queen's House at **Lyndhurst** at intervals of about six weeks. The Verderers control the common rights and look after the Commoners' animals in the New Forest.

The Trafalgar Day ceremonies at **Portsmouth** on October 21st include a service on board H.M.S. *Victory* when a wreath is laid on the spot where Nelson fell.

Southampton preserves several old traditions. The first day of May is greeted by carols, which used to be sung from the top of the Bargate; since the revival of this event ten years ago the choir of King Edward VI school sing on the South Lawn of the Bargate. The eight hundred years old Rogationtide ceremony of the Blessing of the Waters was revived in 1950. A procession of clergy, civic dignitaries and others makes its way to the Ocean Dock for a short service. The blessing is made from a small craft moored close inshore. A second service is held on the Town Quay.

In August a bowls tournament, inaugurated in 1776 and played annually ever since, takes place for the Knighthood of Southampton Old Green. It usually lasts three days and is supervised by the Knights of the Green, who appear in ceremonial dress wearing their medals of rank which are inscribed *Win it and wear it*. The original rules are still observed.

Stockbridge also retains its Courts Leet and Baron which meet annually in the spring. The Courts control grazing on the Marsh: amongst other officers appointed is a hayward whose duties include looking after the common ground.

On October 7th 1753 William Davies became lost in the fog while returning home to **Twyford**; when he heard the bells of the church he changed his direction and thus avoided falling down a chalkpit. In his will he made provision for a feast for the Twyford bellringers in perpetuity, provided that the bells are rung morning and evening on this date; this custom has been observed without a break except for the two wars. The feast is now paid for by the Shipley estates.

The famous "Wayfarer's Dole" is still distributed daily to all who ask at the gatehouse of the Hospital of St. Cross in **Winchester.** For over eight hundred years travellers have received a small square of bread and a drink of ale, until the day's supply has been used.

HEREFORD AND WORCESTER

Members of the **Fownhope** Heart of Oak Friendly Society meet annually on Oak Apple Day (May 29th) or the following Saturday and parade to the church carrying their club sticks which are decorated with wooden oak apples and flowers.

To encourage the residents of **Hentland, Sellack** and **King's Capel** near Ross-on-Wye to live together in peace and goodwill, Lady Scudamore made provision in her sixteenth century will for them to partake of cakes and ale communally on Palm Sunday. Ale is no longer provided, but the lady's wishes are still observed by the distribution of Pax Cakes to the congregation. Each cake bears an impression of the Paschal Lamb and is handed to the parishioners at the end of the service on Palm Sunday with the traditional greeting "God and Good Neighbourhood".

The four hundred year old Winbury Dole Distribution takes place after morning service on New Year's Day at **Castlemorton,** when cake is distributed. The fund of ten shillings per annum derives from a charge on a field near Druggers Lane End. Another bequest provides for the **Kidderminster** Feast of Peace and Good Neighbourhood which still takes place annually. It originated in the fifteenth century when an unknown maiden lady left a bequest of forty shillings to the inhabitants of Church Street "to be put out to interest to provide farthing loaves for the people of the street" and to enable the men to meet once a year to settle their differences peaceably. Three hundred years later a further £150 was bequeathed to provide plum cake, pipes, tobacco and ale for the men at their midsummer gathering.

HUMBERSIDE

The ancient **Haxey** Hood Game is played annually on January 6th. It originated in the thirteenth century when the hood of Lady de Mowbray was retrieved by twelve labourers when it blew away as she was riding home from church. This so amused her Ladyship that she gave a piece of land, still known as the Hoodlands, to the village; the rent was to pay for a leather hood to be contested for annually for ever by twelve men dressed in scarlet. The game, as it is played today, resembles a debased form of rugby football; it is organised and supervised by twelve men known as "Boggans", a "King" and a "Fool" all of whom wear colourful costumes. After the opening ceremonies a canvas "hood" is thrown to the crowd; the person who secures this, eludes the Boggans and takes it to the nearest inn, receives one shilling. After twelve hoods are thus disposed of, the thirteenth, made of leather, is thrown. A general melée ensues and eventually this hood, too, reaches one of the local inns; the game is over, free drinks are dispensed and the hood remains here until the next year.

At **Market Weighton** on the third Thursday in March a horse race, said to be the oldest in England if not in the world, takes place. The Kiplingcotes Derby, which has been held every year since 1519, is run over a four mile course passing through five parishes and finishing near Kiplingcotes Farm. Riders, who must be over ten stone in weight, are weighed on a coal merchant's scale; the prize money for second place is larger than that for the winner.

ISLE OF MAN

The Tynwald ceremony occurs on or about July 5th. There is a service in St. John's church, **Peel,** after which the Lieutenant-Governor leads a procession of officials up a hill said to be made of earth from all the island's seventeen parishes. From the top the island laws are proclaimed in Manx and English. This ceremony must be observed before any of the laws made by the Tynwald—the island parliament—become effective.

Between the 5th and 15th of July, depending on the state of the tides, the **Peel** Viking festival is held. This is an enactment of the conquest of the island by the Vikings; "Vikings" land from longships, there is a battle between them and the "Celts" in which the "Vikings" triumph. A king is elected and there is a torchlight procession and firework display.

KENT

Eliza and Mary Chulkhurst were Siamese twins who lived at **Biddenden.** When they died they left a bequest of twenty acres of land, the income from which was to be used for a distribution of bread and cheese to the poor. This Dole is still distributed on Easter Monday morning; in addition **Bid-**

denden cakes, a variety of hard biscuit stamped with an impression of the two sisters and the year 1100, are available for all who ask for them. The date of birth of these ladies is in dispute and though the cakes are stamped 1100, the year 1500 is thought by some to be a more probable date.

The tolling of the great bell, known as "Bell Harry", occurs daily at **Canterbury** at 9 p.m. On ceremonial occasions the thirteenth century Burghmote Horn, formerly used to summon the citizens to assemblies and meetings, is sounded before the Mayor speaks. Every weekday at 11 a.m. a soldier turns a leaf of one of the books bearing the names of the fallen of the Royal East Kent Regiment. These are kept in the Warrior's Chapel (St. Michael's) in the Cathedral.

The annual Blessing of the Sea service at **Folkestone** takes place in July. At **Margate** a similar service is held in January by the local Greek community to celebrate Epiphany. The Greek Orthodox Archbishop of Thyateria and Great Britain takes part. During the service a crucifix decorated with flowers, which is thrown into the water, is retrieved by a hardy bather.

Hythe Venetian Festival has been held every second year since 1854 on a half mile stretch of the Military Canal, to commemorate the Napoleonic invasion which never occurred in 1804-1805. There is a ceremonial progress of the Mayors of the Cinque Ports Federation on a pontoon accompanied by decorated floats.

The ceremony of the Blessing of the Cherry Orchards, which occurs at **Newington** near Sittingbourne every May, is of comparatively recent origin. There is a service of dedication in the church; then the congregation proceeds to a nearby orchard where the actual Blessing takes place.

The popular medieval sport of Tilting the Quintain now only survives at **Offham**. The Quintain is in permanent position on the village green and consists of a post provided with a sandbag which swings round to strike the unskilful tilter. At the May Day celebrations, in addition to Maypole dancing this spectacle may be witnessed. The tilters are mounted on horseback and a bucket of water replaces the sandbag.

The Mayor of the City of **Rochester** was appointed Admiral of the river Medway in 1446 by Royal Charter and in this capacity he carries out certain duties. Once a year on the first Saturday in July the Admiralty Court, which was established by Act of Parliament in 1728 and is concerned with the administration of the Oyster Fisheries, meets in a decorated barge moored off the Pier. The Mayor attends and walks in procession with civic and other dignitaries, fully robed, from the Guildhall to the barge and returns after the Court has closed.

A service each 24th August in St. Bartholomew's chapel, **Sandwich**, is followed by a distribution of buns and biscuits for which the children have to run around the outside of the chapel. This custom is at least eighty years old.

The Blessing of the Sea at **Whitstable** takes place in August at the water's edge at Reeves Beach. The clergy and choir walk in procession from the parish church.

LANCASHIRE AND GREATER MANCHESTER

The Saturday before Easter in **Bacup** is the venue for the Nutters' Dance performed by the Britannia Coconut Dancers. Eight men attired in black except for white stockings, kilts and caps, and with small wooden discs (the nuts) attached to their waists, hands and knees, dance their way through the town clapping the nuts to a musical accompaniment. The origin of this event is obscure.

The annual Mayor Making Ceremony at **Clitheroe** in May is a colourful occasion as members and officers of the Council walk in procession from a local hostelry, where they assemble, to the Town Hall; the Town Sergeant in his red robes goes from school to school ringing his bell and declaring a holiday for the children. The traditional Cockle and Mussel Feast is held in the same month after the election of councillors, prior to the annual meeting. This feast has taken place for several hundred years and apparently originated in the days when people from the coast brought shellfish to exchange for local products. Nowadays it provides an opportunity for old and new councillors to meet informally before the first council meeting; as it takes place in May tinned shellfish have to be used, but before 1948, when the elections were held in November, fresh ones were consumed, as they were at the original Feasts.

The first recorded perambulation of the Bounds of **Lancaster** took place in 1774; this is now a septennial event next due in 1984. It used to take place on the Wednesday following Whit Monday, but in future it may be the Wednesday following Spring Bank Holiday Monday. Nowadays the complete circuit is made by the Flagman and his Companion; the Mayor and other officials go in procession to meet them at five of the boundary points, where the Mayor makes the customary declaration. In July at the annual Admission of Freemen those eligible swear an oath of allegiance to the Crown and obedience to the Mayor and Magistrates. Complete records of the Roll of Freemen exist for over three hundred years.

The Travice Dole is distributed on Maundy Thursday at **Leigh**. Forty poor people come to the tomb of Henry Travice to receive five shillings each.

Manchester's Whit Walks are probably the best known of all the religious walks which became a feature of north country life in the last century. In 1969 the Roman Catholic Walk occurred on Whit Sunday and the Church of England Walk on Spring Bank Holiday Monday. Both are gala occasions with bands and banners forming part of the huge processions.

Preston is famous for its egg rolling in Avenham Park on Easter Monday. Every twentieth year since 1562 the Preston Guild Merchant has been held for a week in early September. The balls, banquets and civic parades are only incidental to the historic ceremonies of the Guild Court which are still maintained. Because of the war it did not take place in 1942, but 1952 saw its revival.

LEICESTERSHIRE

On St. Peter's Day—June 29th—rushes are spread on the floor of the church at **Barrowden.** Certain fields were left to the church many years ago, the rents from which are for the upkeep of the church; the proviso for the tenant is that he must provide rushes for spreading on the floor on St. Peter's Day otherwise his tenancy is forfeit. Recently some of the ceremonies which attach to this custom elsewhere, notably in the Lake District, were revived here. Hay is scattered on the floor of the church at **Langham** on the Sunday following St. Peter's day.

On the Sunday nearest June 29th, known locally as Hay Sunday, the floor of **Braunstone** church is strewn with hay. Local legend relates that a one time Lord of the Manor made a hay legacy to the parish clerk as a reward for finding his daughter. This entitled the clerk to take the hay from Holm Meadow, Aylestone, and lay it in the church. Today this meadow lies under a local gas works, but the East Midlands Gas Board makes an annual payment in lieu of the hay.

The Nag's Head Inn, **Enderby,** on Whit Monday is the venue for the ancient custom of Selling the Wether. This dates from the fourteenth century when John of Gaunt was passing through the village and joined in the villagers' games. Before he left he gave them a piece of land known as the Wether to be sold annually to provide money for a feast after the sports, and this land is still auctioned. A silver crown is passed round a circle of those taking part in the bidding and bids may only be made when the crown is held. When two circuits have been made without any further bids, the last bidder has the Wether for the next year; after the auction boar's head sandwiches are consumed and church warden pipes are smoked.

At **Glenfield** new hay is laid down in the church on the Thursday after July 6th.

At **Hallaton** Bottle Kicking and Hare Pie Scramble on Easter Monday slices of hare pie, blessed by the vicar, are thrown to the crowd at Hare Pie Bank. Then three small casks, two of which are filled with beer, are kicked or man-handled by teams from Hallaton and nearby Medbourne in an attempt to get them across their own boundary.

In 1786 William Hubbard left one guinea a year forever to the church choir of St. Mary in Arden, **Market Harborough** on condition they sang the Easter Hymn over his grave on Easter Eve. This hymn singing still takes place in the churchyard of the now derelict church.

The first time a Peer of the Realm passes through **Oakham** he is required to present a horseshoe, or the money to have one made, to the Lord of the Manor. There is a remarkable collection of these shoes in the castle including one purporting to have been left by Elizabeth I, and one presented by the present Queen in 1967.

The custom of selling the grass verges for grazing cattle, sheep and horses has taken place at the Gate Inn, **Ratcliffe Culey,** on the Thursday in Easter week for many years; this is known as "spring setting the lanes".

An annual distribution of oranges is made by the vicar on the Sunday School anniversary, usually towards the end of May, under the old elm tree in **Sileby** churchyard. The origin of this custom is obscure, but it is thought to be a revival of an ancient distribution.

At **Whetstone** there is a Rogationtide procession and Blessing on the fifth Sunday after Easter.

LINCOLNSHIRE

On Mayor's Sunday in May there is a civic service in St. Botolph's church, **Boston,** attended by the Mayor and others. In the procession to the church the Mayor is accompanied by three mace bearers and three halberdiers. Afterwards at a reception a traditional toast to the Mayor and Mayoress is proposed by the local Member of Parliament. On December 10th each year the Beast Mart is proclaimed under a charter granted to the Corporation in 1573 by Elizabeth I. The proclamation takes place at noon in the playground of the local grammar school where the Mart was formerly held. It is read by the Town Clerk in the presence of the Mayor and the pupils are granted a half-holiday, symbolic of the times when the school had to be closed during the Mart.

A curious race has been run at **Bourne** every Easter since 1770. In that year Richard Clay left a piece of land to be let each year, the rent from which was to provide bread for the poor. A number of boys race over a fixed distance; as soon as they set off an auctioneer invites bids from people who wish to rent the field. These have to be made while the boys are running, and the last bid before the boys return to the starting point is the successful one.

A strange will made by an inn landlord at **Grantham** provided the sum of forty shillings per annum for ever for an annual sermon to be preached "wherein the subject shall be chiefly against drunkenness"; it is still delivered under the terms of his bequest on the evening of Mayor's Sunday.

Up till 1938 the grazing rights of a field known as "Poor Folks' Close" in **Old Bolingbroke** were let annually by pin and candle auction and the proceeds distributed to the poor on St. Thomas's Day. This land is now administered in a different manner, but the tradition of the Candle Auction continues, for when the King George V Playing Field was left to the Parish Council it was specified that the grazing on this land should be let annually by the ancient method. A pin is placed in a candle not more than one inch from the top, the candle is lit and bidding for the grazing commences; whoever makes the last bid before the pin falls is accepted as the purchaser. This auction takes place at the annual Parish Assembly in March.

LONDON

Royal Events

The Sovereign or her representative, accompanied by the Yeomen of the Guard, attends the Royal Epiphany Service at the Chapel Royal, St. James, on January 6th. Three purses, symbolising the gifts of the three Wise Men, are presented and afterwards their contents are distributed to the poor of the parish.

On the Thursday before Good Friday the Royal Maundy Money, specially minted for the occasion, is distributed by the Sovereign. This used to take place in Westminster Abbey, but recently a different church elsewhere in the country has been chosen each year.

At the Trooping the Colour on the second Saturday in June (the Queen's official birthday) the Colours of one of the five Foot Guards' Regiments are trooped before the Queen on Horse Guards Parade. Afterwards the Queen rides to Buckingham Palace at the head of her Guards.

The first Royal Tournament was held in 1880. This annual event takes place at Earls Court in July and branches of all three services present displays.

After a general election and before each new session of Parliament in mid-November the Queen attends the State Opening of Parliament, a ceremony dating from the mid-sixteenth century. She travels in procession from Buckingham Palace to the Palace of Westminster where she reads the speech from the Throne of the House of Lords. A few hours before this, the cellars of the Houses of Parliament are searched by the Beefeaters to ensure no Guy Fawkes lurks there.

Royal Salutes of 41 guns are fired in Hyde Park by the King's Troop of the Royal Horse Artillery and at the Tower by the Honourable Artillery Company, who fire an additional 21 guns for the City of London. These salutes are fired on various occasions throughout the year:— the anniversary of the Accession—February 6th, the Queen's Birthday—April 21st, the Coronation anniversary—June 2nd, the Duke of Edinburgh's birthday—June 10th, the Queen's official birthday—the second Saturday in June, and the Queen Mother's birthday—August 4th.

On state occasions when the Sovereign has to enter the City of London she is met at the City Boundary—Temple Bar—by the Lord Mayor, who surrenders the Keys of the City to her before she proceeds.

Daily Events

The changing of the Guard at Buckingham Palace occurs at 11.30 a.m. The Guard, accompanied by a band, marches from Wellington or Chelsea Barracks, and the band plays in the forecourt while the Guard is changed. Mounting the Guard at Whitehall takes place at 11 a.m. on weekdays and 10 a.m. on Sundays.

The Bank Guard or "Picquet", instituted in 1780, is mounted daily at the Bank of England at 4.30 p.m., but as the soldiers arrive by coach there is little ceremony to see.

The Ceremony of the Keys takes place in the Tower at about 9.50 p.m. The Chief Warder locks up the Tower for the night and conveys the Keys to the Resident Governor; Last Post is sounded. Permission to attend this event may be obtained at the Constable's office.

Weekly Events

On Saturdays at 9.00 a.m. at Fern Street Settlement in Tower Hamlets "Farthing Bundles" are distributed to children small enough to pass under an archway inscribed *Enter now ye children small, None can come who are too tall.* In return for a penny the children receive "bundles" of small toys or trinkets.

Annual Events

January 6th—The cast at Drury Lane Theatre consume cake and wine as directed in the will of the comedian Baddeley, who died in 1795.

January 8th or the first Sunday after—The Chaplain of Clowns preaches a sermon and recites a prayer over the grave of Grimaldi, the clown, at St. James's church, Pentonville ; a wreath is laid.

January 30th—Wreaths are laid on the statue of Charles I at Charing Cross to mark the anniversary of his execution.

February 3rd—St. Blaise, whose festival this is, is the patron saint of throats. At the church of St. Etheldreda, Holborn, the ceremony of Blessing the Throats has taken place for over one hundred years.

February 20th—The annual memorial service for Sir John Cass is held on or near this day at St. Botolph's church, Aldgate. He died of a haemorrhage while making his will

1. Avon: The costume of one of the Marshfield mummers is exhibited at Castle Farm Folk Museum, Marshfield, near Chippenham.

2. *London: Druids welcome the Equinox of Spring on Tower Hill.*

3. *London: Cutting the Knollys rose for presentation by the churchwardens of All Hallows by the Tower to the Lord Mayor.*

4. London: The Royal Horse Artillery fire a Royal Salute in Hyde Park.

5. London: The Quit Rent payment of nails and horseshoes at the Law Courts.

6. Derbyshire: The centrepiece from one of the well-dressing tableaux at Bradwell.

7. Cornwall: The Helston Furry Dance.

8. Shropshire: Children process through Aston-on-Clun in the Arbor Day ceremony.

9. Cumbria: Rushbearing on Peter Day at Warcop; the girls carry garlands, the boys rushes.

10. Hertfordshire: A pancake race on Shrove Tuesday at the village of Wigginton.

11. Devon: Tip-toeing at Gittisham on Shrove Tuesday.

12. Oxfordshire: The Headington Quarry Morris Men in their distinctive blue caps.

13. Wiltshire: The Grovely procession at Wishford.

in 1718, and scholars of Sir John Cass College attending the service wear red quills in his memory.

Shrove Tuesday—At Westminster School "Pancake Greaze" a pancake is tossed over a bar and boys scramble for a piece; the one who obtains the largest receives a reward.

Ash Wednesday—Under a bequest in the 1612 will of John Norton, members of the Stationers' Company process from Stationers' Hall to St. Faith's Chapel in the Crypt of St. Paul's to hear a special sermon. On returning to their Hall they partake of cakes and ale.

March 14th—At the Trial of the Pyx coins from the Mint are sent to Goldsmiths' Hall where they are tested for weight and fineness by a jury of members of the Goldsmiths' Company.

Mothering Sunday—At a revival of a ceremony dating from Tudor times, young persons receive flowers and Simnel cakes at a service in the Chapel Royal at the Tower.

March 21st—Druids meet on Tower Hill to celebrate the Spring Equinox.

March 28th—The bells of St. Clement Danes church were restored in 1919 and to commemorate this a service is held at 3 p.m., followed by a distribution of oranges and lemons to the children present.

April 5th—A memorial service to John Stow, attended by the Lord Mayor and Aldermen, is held in the church of St. Andrew Undershaft on or near the anniversary of his death. A new quill is placed in the hand of Stow's statue during the service.

Good Friday—After a morning service in the church of St. Bartholomew the Great, Smithfield, twenty-one widows of the parish collect a bun and sixpence from the top of the tomb in the churchyard.

The Widow's Son Inn, Bow, recalls Good Friday years ago when a widow's son was expected home from sea. She put a Hot Cross bun aside for him; he never came but she continued to keep one for him every year. A bun is now added every year to the collection hanging from a bag in the bar, and there is a general distribution of buns to patrons of the inn.

2nd Wednesday after Easter—At a special service in the church of St. Lawrence Jewry the annual Spital sermon, preached since before the Fire of London, is delivered by a Diocesan Bishop nominated by the Archbishop of Canterbury. The Lord Mayor and Aldermen attend.

Last Sunday—A Roman Catholic pilgrimage, following the route taken by victims from Newgate prison (Old Bailey) to Tyburn Gallows (Marble Arch), commemorates the martyrs of religious persecution in the sixteenth and seventeenth centuries.

May: Ascension Day—When the Bounds of St. Clement Danes parish are beaten one of the boundaries in the river Thames has to be reached by boat, and one of the choirboys is lowered by his heels to reach a mark in Temple Gardens.

Every second year (1981, 1983, etc.) the Bounds of the Manor and Liberty of the Savoy are beaten, following a service in the Queen's Chapel of the Savoy at 10.45 a.m. During the procession one of the choristers stands on his head several times.

Every third year (1981, 1984) the Bounds of the Tower are beaten. After a service at 6 p.m. in the Chapel Royal of St. Peter Ad Vincula a colourful procession makes its way round the thirty-one boundary marks. The choirboys strike each one with willow wands.

May 21st—Henry VI was murdered in the Tower on this date in 1471 and each year representatives from Eton College and King's College, Cambridge process to the Wakefield Tower, where the murder occurred, and lay lilies and red roses on the spot.

Last Wednesday—At noon in the church of St. Olave, Hart Street, at the annual Pepys' Commemoration Service a laurel wreath is laid in front of the diarist's memorial.

May 29th—This is Oak Apple Day and Founders Day at the Chelsea Royal Hospital. The Pensioners parade for inspection in their colourful uniforms and all wear a sprig of oak. They give three cheers for their founder, Charles II, whose statue is decorated with oak boughs.

June: Thursday after Trinity Sunday—Members of the Skinners' Company walk in procession from Skinners' Hall, Dowgate Hill, to the church of St. Mary Aldermanbury. The procession includes the Master, members of the Court, the Beadles and boys from Christ's Hospital, all of whom carry posies.

Midsummer Day—An annual fine was imposed on Sir Robert Knollys in 1346 when he built a small bridge over Seething Lane, to connect two of his properties, without planning permission (even in those days). He was ordered to present a red rose personally to the Lord Mayor on this day each year. In 1924 this payment was revived and the churchwardens of All Hallows by the Tower present a red rose to the Lord Mayor every year.

The Election of two Sheriffs and other officials of the City takes place at Guildhall with much pageantry. The Lord Mayor and other city officials attend a church service before proceeding to the Guildhall where members of the Livery Companies are assembled.

July: Thursday after the 4th—The Vinters' Company process from their Hall in Upper Thames Street to the church of St. James, Garlickhythe for a service. A wine porter dressed in top hat and smock heads the procession, sweeping the path clear with a birch broom. This occurs at about noon.

July 10th—Members of the Grocers' Company attend a service in their Company's church following the election of Company officials.

Third week—Swan Upping and Marking of the swans of the River Thames is performed by the Queen's Swanmaster and the Swanmasters of the Dyers' and Vintners' Companies over a period of about a week. These Companies and the Queen between them own all the swans on the river from London Bridge to Henley-on-Thames, and the birds are counted and marked appropriately.

Towards the end—The race for Doggett's Coat and Badge occurs on a variable date depending on the state of the tides. This event was instituted in 1716 by an Irish actor—Thomas Doggett—and he made provision in his will for it to be an annual event. There are six finalists, and the race is rowed over a four and a half mile course from London Bridge to Cadogan Pier, Chelsea. The winner receives an orange coat with a large silver badge on the sleeve.

September 21st or thereabouts—Boys from Christ's Hospital, Horsham march from London Bridge Station to St. Sepulchre's church, High Holborn for a service at about 11 a.m. Afterwards they go to the Mansion House where they are received by the Lord Mayor. They are accompanied by the school band.

September 23rd or thereabouts—A Druid ceremony is held on Parliament Hill Fields at mid-day to celebrate the Autumn Equinox.

September 28th—The Sheriffs elected in June take office at a ceremony in Guildhall; the Lord Mayor, Alderman and others go from the Mansion House to attend this event.

September 29th—The election of the Lord Mayor takes place at noon; the Lord Mayor goes to the Guildhall for the election of his successor, walks in procession from Guildhall to the Church of St. Lawrence Jewry and returns across Guildhall Yard.

October: First Sunday—At 11 a.m. the Harvest of the Sea Thanksgiving Service is held in the church of St. Mary-at-Hill, Lovat Lane.

At 3 p.m. the Costermongers' Harvest Festival, held at St. Martin's-in-the-Fields, is attended by the Pearly Kings and Queens in full costume.

October 16th or near—The Lion sermon is preached annually at the church of St. Katherine Cree, Leadenhall Street, traditionally at 1.15 p.m. to commemorate the deliverance of a London merchant—Sir John Gayer—from a lion when he was travelling in Arabia. He was buried in the church in 1694 and left money for this annual sermon.

October 21st—The Battle of Trafalgar is commemorated, and wreaths are laid at the foot of Nelson's Column in Trafalgar Square.

October 21st (about)—The Quit Rents' Ceremony takes place at the Law Courts. The City Solicitor pays the Queen's Remembrancer a bill-hook, a hatchet and two faggots of wood for some land in Shropshire called the Moors, though the whereabouts of this land is lost to posterity. The second payment consists of six horseshoes and sixty-one nails, paid annually since 1234 for the site of an old forge near St. Clement Dane's church.

Last Wednesday—Officials of the Worshipful Company of Basketmakers attend a special service at the church of St. Margaret Pattens, Eastcheap at noon.

November: Second Saturday—The Lord Mayor, elected in September, takes office. He travels by coach from Guildhall to the Law Courts where he takes the oath at noon before the Lord Chief Justice, returning by coach after the ceremony. His coach forms only one part of a procession of decorated floats and lorries all having a common theme which varies from year to year. Known as the Lord Mayor's Show this popular event is over six hundred years old and attracts great crowds.

December: Wednesday before Christmas—A Boar's Head Feast, similar to that at Oxford, is held by the Worshipful

Company of Cutlers, at Warwick Lane.

Near to Christmas—Under instructions issued in 1691 the Chelsea Pensioners receive a piece of cheese and a tankard of beer.

NORFOLK

Bede House, **Castle Rising,** is a hospital for widows and spinsters founded by the Howard family in 1614 and the distinctive dress of the occupants—red cloaks and Jacobean hats—may still be seen when they attend church on Sundays.

At **Cawston** there is an annual Plough Sunday service, usually held a few weeks after January 6th; the future of a similar service which has been held at **Hedenham** each year is uncertain.

At the opening of the **King's Lynn** Mart, traditionally performed by the Mayor in his chain of office, he is accompanied by the Sword Bearer and Mace Bearers in uniform, and mayors of other East Anglian towns also attend.

In medieval times many pilgrimages were made to the Shrine of Our Lady at **Walsingham**; the Anglican shrine at the new church built in 1931 and the Roman Catholic shrine just outside the village are still visited by pilgrims throughout the summer. Of particular note are the pilgrimages to the Anglican shrine at Whitsun, and to the Roman Catholic shrine on the first Thursday in July and again at Assumption-tide (August 15th and the following Sunday).

At the church of St. Mary, **Wiveton Green,** every Saturday afternoon there is a short ceremony when several pensioners receive five shillings each under the will of Ralph Greneway who died in 1558.

NORTHAMPTONSHIRE

Broughton Tin Can Band, formed in the Middle Ages to cast out gipsies, may still be heard once a year. The performance commences at midnight on the second Sunday after St. Andrew's Day—November 30th. A group of about sixty players march through the streets banging on tin cans and buckets, and this cacophony lasts for about an hour.

The Pole Fair, or Charter Fair, takes place at **Corby** every twenty years on Spring Bank Holiday Monday. The next is due in 1982.

At **Flore** near Weedon the May Day celebrations are led by the school and a floral crown made by the children is carried round the village on two long poles before the crowning of the May Queen.

Oak Apple Day (May 29th) is marked in **Northampton** by the placing of a wreath of oak leaves on the statue of Charles II in All Saints' church. This commemorates a gift of wood which the king made to the town for rebuilding, after most of it had been destroyed in a great fire in 1675.

NORTHUMBERLAND

At **Allendale** the New Year is welcomed in spectacular fashion by men in fancy dress who process through the streets carrying containers of burning tar on their heads. The barrels are thrown on an unlit bonfire just before midnight to ignite it, and as midnight strikes all present dance round singing *Auld Lang Syne*. Then the men go first-footing in the traditional way. This bonfire probably originated in rites performed to celebrate the winter solstice.

Shrove Tuesday at **Alnwick** is the scene of a game of Shrovetide football. The game, between the parishes of St. Michael and St. Paul, is no longer played through the village streets, but in a field. The ball is piped on to the pitch by the Duke of Northumberland's Piper, kick off is at 2.30 p.m. and the ball may not be handled. The goals are a quarter of a mile apart, teams may contain over 150 people and after a total of three goals have been scored the game ceases; the ball is thrown in the air and the person who manages to carry it off the pitch retains it.

The historic town of **Berwick-upon-Tweed** maintains several old traditions. Curfew is rung each night, except Sunday, at 8 p.m. and the Pancake Bell is rung on Shrove Tuesday. The Mayor and other officials perambulate the boundaries on horseback annually on May Day; parts of the boundary inspected include some of the Scottish-English border. The year 1945 saw the revival of the Crowning of the Salmon Queeen at nearby **Tweedmouth.**

Several traditional bells are rung at **Morpeth,** including Curfew nightly at 8.00 p.m. and the Market Bell on Wednesdays. The riding of the borough boundaries takes place at irregular but frequent intervals. This event used to take place on St. Mark's Day—April 25th—and was followed by races in which the Burgesses competed for a piece of plate given by the magistrates.

The Walking of the Bounds at **Newbiggin-by-the-Sea** has been practised since 1235 and now takes place annually on the Wednesday nearest May 18th. During the walk new Freeholders are initiated by allowing themselves to be bumped three times on a boundary stone known as the Dunting Stone on Newbiggin Moor. Nuts and raisins are scattered after the ceremony.

On February 14th on Pedwell Beach at **Norham** the vicar blesses the nets at the opening of the salmon fishing season; all present repeat the ancient Pedwell prayer, and the first net is cast and drawn. The officiating priest receives the first salmon caught.

The ceremonial fire, known as the Baal or Bale Fire, which is lit at **Whalton** on July 4th (Old Midsummer Eve) is probably a relic of pagan midsummer rites. In olden times villagers used to leap through the flames; nowadays children dance round and sweets are distributed.

NORTH YORKSHIRE

From September 27th until Shrove Tuesday a horn is sounded nightly at nine o'clock on **Bainbridge** village green; this custom is seven hundred years old.

Several customs are still observed at **Richmond.** The Apprentice and Curfew Bells are rung at 8 a.m. and 8 p.m. respectively; the Pancake Bell is rung on Shrove Tuesday and the Passing Bell as appropriate. Every year on a variable date in September (usually the first Saturday) the Mayor, as Clerk of the Market, presents a bottle of wine to the first local farmer who brings to the Market Cross a "respectable sample of the new season's wheat", the First Fruits of the Harvest. This wine is used to drink the Mayor's health and the farmer receives a second bottle to take home. Every seventh year the Bounds are beaten. The Mayor and various officials make a fifteen mile circuit of the boundary which used to include a wade in the river Swale; this wet task is now performed by only one person—the Water Wader. New pennies are distributed during the perambulation.

The Curfew Horn is sounded each evening at 9 p.m. in the Market Place at **Ripon**; the only one of the five original Horn Days, when the Mayor and other civic officials walked in procession from the Town Hall to the Cathedral with the famous Horn, still observed is St. Wilfrid's Sunday in August. Civic church parades are held on seven other days throughout the year.

The Shrove Tuesday Pancake Bell is rung in **Scarborough** and Shrovetide skipping (a relic of an old Shrovetide fair) takes place on the foreshore in the afternoon, when all who wish skip using long ropes provided for the purpose.

Beating the Bounds of the Manor of **Spaunton** involves a thirty mile hike and takes place only occasionally when a new Lord of the Manor takes over the estate.

The Burning of Bartle has taken place at **West Witton** for many years and now occurs on the evening of the Saturday nearest St. Bartholomew's Day in August. Old Bartle was probably a local villain who persistently stole the villagers' swine; when they chased him down the local fellside towards the village he fell and broke his neck, and was finally burnt at the stake in Grassgill Lane. An effigy of Old Bartle is made in great secrecy and carried through the village after dark. The procession stops at intervals to shout a verse retailing the fate of Old Bartle during the chase, and the dummy is finally consigned to the flames in Grassgill Lane.

A Shrove Tuesday Pancake Race, apparently a revival of an old tradition, takes place on the West Pier at **Whitby** and the winner receives a cup. There is a Rogationtide Blessing of the Sea in May and on the morning of the day before Ascension Day the Planting of the Penny Hedge takes place. The story relates that when a hermit gave refuge to a wild boar the angry huntsmen broke into his cell and attacked him; as he died he begged the Abbot of Whitby to show mercy to his attackers if they and their descendants would do penance. They were ordered to erect a hedge of stakes and branches at the water's edge each year strong enough to resist the onslaught of three tides. This hedge is still planted every year.

The famous **York** Mystery Plays originated about 1350 and are now performed triennially in June in the ruins of St. Mary's Abbey. Ringing of the Curfew Bell of St. Michael's church, Spurriergate has been revived recently.

NOTTINGHAMSHIRE

At the church of St. Mary, **Blidworth,** an event believed to be unique in this country takes place on the Sunday nearest February 2nd (the Feast of the Purification of the Blessed

Virgin Mary). Known as the Rocking Ceremony, it was revived by the vicar in 1922 and symbolises the presentation of the young Jesus at the Temple. The most recently baptised male child in the parish, carried by his parents and attended by his god-parents, is formally presented to the priest, who places him in a cradle before the altar. In the course of a short service of dedication the flower-bedecked cradle is rocked by the priest several times before the child is handed back to his parents as the *Nunc Dimittis* is sung.

Laxton is the only English village where the ancient open field system of farming has survived practically unchanged since the Norman Conquest. Agricultural matters are governed by the Court Leet which meets annually in December. A jury appointed by the Court carries out an inspection of the winter cornfield every November to ensure that everything is in order. Fines for mismanagement are collected at the Court meeting.

The annual Gopher ringing at **Newark** commemorates a Flemish merchant named Gopher who, lost in the marshes round the town, was guided to safety by the Newark bells. He left some money for the church bells to be rung on the five Sundays before Christmas.

The Luke Jackson sermons have been preached annually in St. Peter's church, **Nottingham**, since 1631; a Gunpowder sermon is preached on the Sunday nearest November 5th and an Armada sermon on the Sunday nearest July 28th.

Records of Maypole dancing at **Wellow** (now held on Spring Bank Holiday Monday) extend back to the beginning of the nineteenth century. The 65-foot Maypole, topped by its golden weathercock and vane, is a permanent feature of the village green.

OXFORDSHIRE

At **Abingdon,** in addition to the Election of the Mayor of Ock Street around June 20th the custom of Bun Throwing by the Mayor and Corporation is still maintained. Buns similar to hot cross buns are thrown from the top of County Hall to people assembled in the Market Place. There is much competition to obtain a bun and some families have a complete collection of buns from every throwing since the coronation of George III when the custom originated. Bun throwing takes place on occasions of special importance to the town.

Bampton claims to be the original home of the Great Shirt Race, which celebrated an occasion in 784 when Ethelred the Shirtless chased the Burghers of the town through the streets in an unsuccessful attempt to clothe himself. This event was revived in 1952 and takes place on Spring Bank Holiday Monday, when there is also Morris Dancing. The Bampton Morris Ring is said to have existed for five hundred years and a Sword Bearer accompanies the dancers. The cake he distributes to the onlookers brings good luck and husbands for the girls.

In the church at **Charlton-in-Otmoor** a cross covered with box branches, known locally as the May Garland, stands on the screen throughout the year. The greenery is renewed for May Day and for the dedication festival in September. At 9 a.m. on May Day or on the nearest school day the children walk from the school to the church carrying a long garland decorated with leaves and flowers. Each child also makes and brings a small cross decorated with flowers; before they enter church they sing the May Garland song. In church the garland is hung on the screen, there is a short service and the two best crosses are hung over the church door to be left until they fade. Before they return to school the children dance in the streets outside the church. Before 1963 the children used to carry their small crosses from house to house singing a little song and asking for pennies.

A traditional Mumming Play is performed at **Headington** at Christmas each year. Several old customs are preserved at **Oxford.** After dinner on New Year's Day the Bursar of Queen's College presents every Fellow with a needle and coloured thread, saying "Take it and be thrifty", thus fulfilling the terms of an old bequest. On Ascension Day after a service in St. Michael's church the bounds of the parish are beaten; choirboys and others who assist in the ceremonies receive hot pennies after a traditional lunch at Lincoln College.

The Hymn of Thanksgiving—the *Te Deum Patrem Collimus* written about 1600—is always included in the May Day Carols which are sung from the top of Magdalen College Tower at 6 a.m. on May 1st. After the singing the College bells ring out and there is Morris dancing in the High. On the Sunday after St. John the Baptist's Day (June 24th) the Wall Pulpit sermon is preached from an open air pulpit in the first quadrangle at Magdalen College, commemorating the fact that a Hospital of St. John the Baptist once stood on the site. The Simon Perrot Oration is given on the first Monday of the Trinity Term at Magdalen College. At the Boar's Head ceremony at Queen's College in December a boar's head is carried in as part of the Christmas fare. The Provost, Dons and Fellows are summoned by blowing an ancient hunting horn and as the head is carried in the traditional carol is sung in Latin.

On 23rd April takes place the Shakespeare Memorial Ceremony. The Mayor and civic officials go in procession to the Painted Room in the Cornmarket, Oxford, and drink the poet's health in sack and malmsey. This room once formed part of New College property and was called the Crown Tavern. The landlord was John Davenant, later mayor of Oxford, and father of the poet Sir William Davenant, Shakespeare's godson. The family were close friends of Shakespeare's and Aubrey recorded that Shakespeare often stayed here on the journey between Stratford and London.

In 1965, after a lapse of about 200 years, there was a revival of "Clipping the Church" at **Radley** on Easter Sunday.

At **Shenington** near Banbury grass is strewn in Holy Trinity Church annually on Whit Saturday and renewed the following Saturday.

An apprentice bell is tolled daily at 6 a.m. and the curfew nightly at 9 p.m. at **Wallingford.** This latter is said to have originated in the time of William I, who granted Wallingford a later curfew than that imposed upon the rest of England because the town allowed him unimpeded passage when he crossed the Thames there on his way from Hastings to London.

SHROPSHIRE

The Arbor Tree at **Aston-on-Clun** is decked with flags on May 29th and local children walk through the village in seventeenth century costume. In 1660 Charles II declared May 29th as Arbor Day, a national holiday on which trees should be dressed with flags.

SOMERSET

Bridgwater Guy Fawkes Carnival claims an unbroken record since 1605; when the news of the failure of the Gunpowder Plot reached the town, bonfires were lit and impromptu processions were held and except for the war years the celebrations have been repeated annually ever since. Nowadays the Carnival is held on the nearest Thursday to November 5th.

Carhampton on January 17th (Old Twelfth Night) is the scene of a centuries-old custom known as Wassailing the Apple Trees. In order to safeguard the trees and drive away any evil spirits which might harm the apple crops villagers encircle the largest tree in one of the local orchards. The branches are decorated with toast soaked in cider, an incantation is sung, cider is thrown on to the tree and guns are fired into its branches. Then the tree is toasted in cider and a song, urging it to bear much fruit, is sung.

Chedzoy Candle Auction is held every twenty-first year; the next one is due in 1988.

An old custom which has been revived at a **Dunster** hotel is the Burning of the Ashen Faggot on Christmas Eve. The faggot of ash twigs, bound with green ash bands, is burned on an open fire and as each band bursts a round of cider is drunk. Some of the charred remains are retained to ignite the next year's faggot.

At the historic town of **Glastonbury** the Holy Thorn, a descendant of the tree which sprang from a thorn staff plunged into the ground by Joseph of Arimathea, is reputed to flower on Old Christmas Day—January 6th. In fact it may flower at any time in late December or early January, and many people visit the town to see this. It is customary for some sprays to be cut from the tree a few days before Christmas by the Mayor and vicar of the church of St. John the Baptist for dispatch to the Queen.

October 31st, Hallowe'en to most of us, is Punky Night at **Hinton St. George.** Children carve the traditional Hallowe'en lanterns, known here as "Punkies", from mangelwurzels and go through the streets singing; when they knock on doors they receive either money or a candle from the householders. It is said to commemorate an incident when some of the village men were missing and their wives searched for them by the light of lanterns made from mangelwurzels.

Minehead Hobby Horse appears on the streets on the evening of April 30th, on May Day itself and on the following two days. The "Horse", which is a structure over six feet long resembling a bearded horse with a boat-shaped body made of canvas and decorated with ribbons, may represent a survival of ancient fertility rites. But it is also said to recall a shipwreck on May Day Eve, 1722, from which a cow was washed ashore; the tail was cut off, attached to a hobby horse and used to chastise people who refused to pay a toll.

The ancient Shrovetide custom of Egg Shackling survives in the villages of **Stoke St. Gregory** and **Shepton Beauchamp,** where the children take eggs to school on Shrove Tuesday.

These are marked, placed in a sieve and shaken gently; as they crack they are removed and the owner of the last uncracked egg receives a prize. At Stoke St. Gregory the cracked eggs are sent to the local hospital and at Shepton Beauchamp the children take them home for pancakes. This procedure may represent a survival of seasonal rituals practised to promote fertility and drive away evil forces.

At the **Tatworth** Candle Auction, held annually on the Tuesday following the first Saturday after April 6th, a piece of land known as "Spowell Meadow" is let. During the proceedings, at which an inch of candle is used, no one may rise from his seat or speak unless to bid, and the last bid before the candle goes out is the successful one. No pin is used in this case, as it is in some other Candle Auctions.

STAFFORDSHIRE

On the Monday following 4th September **Abbots Bromley** is the scene of the famous Horn Dance which commemorates the granting of hunting rights to the villagers in Needwood Forest. Reindeer heads, which are normally kept in the church, are carried by dancers in Tudor costume so that the horns appear to sprout from their own heads. They dance thoughout the day in the locality of the village accompanied by traditional figures such as Maid Marian, Robin Hood and a Hobby Horse, but the horns are never allowed to leave the parish.

Egg Rolling and a Pace Egg Play take place at **Draycott-in-the-Clay** at the beginning of April. One of the few places outside Derbyshire where there is a well-dressing is **Endon.** It has taken place since 1845 and the crowning of a well-dressing Queen dates from 1868. The event occurs over Spring Bank Holiday Weekend.

The single Warden of **Leek** parish church also holds the ancient office of Warden of Leek. Three nominations for this appointment are made at the Annual Vestry, which all ratepayers may attend, and any ratepayer may be nominated. If there are more than three nominations a town election is held, and in fact this unusual occurrence took place a few years ago.

Lichfield has maintained several ancient customs. At noon on St. George's Day—April 23rd—the Court of View of Frank Pledge and the Court Baron of the Burgesses, otherwise St. George's Court, are held in the Guildhall. The Town Clerk, as Steward of the Manor, presides and a jury is present to hear complaints and to appoint two High Constables, a

Bailiff and other officers. On Ascension Day the ecclesiastical bounds are beaten by cathedral officials. The procession of choir and clergy carries elm boughs and stops at eight places to sing a psalm. On their return to the Cathedral the boughs are placed round the font. On Spring Bank Holiday Monday the Court of Arraye and Court Leet are held. Youths in ancient coats of mail parade for inspection by town officials; this dates from times when freemen were required to have suits of armour and weapons ready for use in war, and these were inspected annually. On the same day the Greenhill Bower takes place; this probably started as a pagan floral rite and in the Middle Ages various craft guilds used to parade. Today there is a floral procession and a fair.

The riding of the City Bounds of Lichfield used to take place in the spring, but under a charter granted by Queen Mary in 1553 the Sheriff had to ride the bounds on the Feast of the Nativity of the Virgin Mary—September 8th; today it usually takes place on the nearest Saturday. Various halts for refreshment are made on the twenty-four mile ride. On the Saturday nearest September 18th the Mayor, Sheriff, members of the Johnson Society and boys from the King Edward VI school walk in procession from the Guildhall to the Market Place where a wreath is laid on Dr. Johnson's statue to commemorate his birthday. At a commemorative supper in the evening Johnson's favourite meal, of steak and kidney pie and apple tart with cream, is served. On December 21st, St. Thomas's Day, every house in the Cathedral Close receives one small loaf provided by the Dean's Vicar.

Uttoxeter also remembers Dr. Johnson's birthday on the Monday following the Lichfield ceremony, when a wreath is fixed to a plaque on the wall of an old stone kiosk in the Market Place. This commemorates an occasion when Johnson, whose father kept a bookstall in the market, stood in the rain there as an act of penance for disobeying an order from his father in his youth.

SUFFOLK

The Cakes and Ale ceremony at **Bury St. Edmunds** commemorates the town's great benefactor, Jankyn Smith. Each of the almshouse residents attending a service in St. Mary's church, at which the oldest endowed sermon in the country is preached, receives one shilling; the trustees, who also attend, then retire to the Guildhall where they partake of cakes and ale (nowadays sherry) and toast his memory. Since the seventeenth century this service has been held in January on the Thursday following Plough Monday, but recent research has shown that Smith died on June 28th 1481, and in future this event will take place on the Thursday nearest the anniversary of his death.

The distribution of Carlow Bread takes place at **Woodbridge** on February 2nd. George Carlow, a local tanner, died in 1783 and was buried in his garden. He left a rent charge of one pound on the property to provide sixty twopenny loaves and six score penny loaves for distribution to the poor on Candlemas Day forever. About twenty loaves are handed out today at his tomb, which is situated in the grounds of the Bull Hotel, whose owner pays the rental.

SURREY

The foundation stone of the almshouses at **Croydon** was laid on March 22nd, 1618 and ever since a Founder's Day service has been held in the parish church every year on this date. It commemorates Archbishop Whitgift, the founder, and is attended by the occupants of the almshouses, masters and boys from the Whitgift School and members of the Fishmongers' Company. A wreath is laid on his tomb.

A ceremony held annually in the Guild Hall, **Guildford** at the end of January or beginning of February is known as Dicing for the Maid's Money. Under the will of John How dated 1674 two long-serving maids within the Borough of Guildford cast dice for the interest on £400 left for this purpose; this amounts to about £12. Under another charity dating from 1704 there is a larger income originally intended for an impoverished apprentice within the Borough. Since no one seems to qualify under the original terms of the second will any more, the Trustees use this money for the runner-up at dice, who therefore benefits more than the winner.

Yet another bequest governs the curious events which take place in the churchyard at **Wotton,** near Dorking every June. William Glanville, who was buried here in 1711, left two pounds to each of five boys of the parish under sixteen years of age provided that they recite the Ten Commandments, the Apostle's Creed and the Lord's Prayer with their hands resting on his tomb. They must also read and write a portion of one of St. Paul's Epistles to the Corinthians. The two boys who gain the highest marks in the competition for these awards receive an additional reward if they are willing to be apprenticed to a trade.

TYNE AND WEAR

A recently created custom, instituted only in 1955, is the presentation of a red rose annually to the Duke of Northumberland or his agent as token rent for a piece of land near the church at **Newburn.** The rent for this land, used as an open space, is paid in August.

On Dookie Apple Night—Hallowe'en—in **Newcastle** children parade the streets carrying the traditional turnip lanterns. Here, too, every seventh year during September is held the traditional auction of leases of the intakes of the Town Moor, by the sand glass method.

At **Seaham Harbour, South Shields** and **Sunderland** it is customary for Sunday school children to walk round the town on Good Friday. The Seaham parade has been held every year since at least 1899 and the Sunderland parade since 1850. At Easter in some parts of the county eggs which have been hard-boiled and dyed are rolled on the grass or "jauped" (thrown) against each other till they break.

WARWICKSHIRE

A Court Leet is held annually at **Alcester.** The **Atherstone** Shrove Tuesday Football game, played with a water-filled ball decorated with the colours of the local football team, lasts only two hours after kick-off at 3 p.m. The game originated in the reign of King John as a contest between men from Warwickshire and Leicestershire for a bag of gold.

The Lord of the Manor—the Duke of Buccleuch—or his agent collects yearly tithes from representatives of various surrounding parishes at **Knightlow Hill** before dawn on the morning of November 11th, St. Martin's Day. After the reading of the Charter of Assembly, each person throws his money, known as Wroth Silver, into the stone base of an old cross; this payment preserves a right to drive cattle across the Duke's land and the penalty for non-payment is a pound for every penny owed. Breakfast is then taken at a local inn.

The Shakespeare Birthday Celebrations at **Stratford upon Avon** on April 23rd make a colourful occasion with flags of many nations flying from decorated poles down the centre of Bridge Street; a procession of townspeople and visitors wends its way to the Bard's grave to lay wreaths.

The first Ascension Day Tower Service was held in **Warwick** in 1907 on the tower of St. Mary's church. Today it is no longer a service as such, but the four Anglican church choirs in the town all sing from different towers in succession, to a planned timetable. A meeting of Warwick Court Leet is held annually in October. It still possesses certain powers concerning St. Mary's Common and appoints four Chamberlains to control matters connected with this land. Bread Weighers, Ale Tasters, Fish and Flesh Tasters, Butter Weighers and Overseers of Pavements, with purely nominal duties, are also appointed.

There is a permanent Maypole on the village green at **Welford-on-Avon** where Maypole dancing has taken place for at least seventy-five years. It usually occurs on the second or third Saturday afternoon in May.

WEST MIDLANDS

The **Coventry** Miracle Plays are still performed from time to time in the ruins of the old cathedral.

The Cyclists' War Memorial at **Meriden** was unveiled on May 21st 1921, and a remembrance service, attended by cyclists from all over the country, has been held here annually since then on the nearest Sunday to this date. The archery meetings of the Woodmen of Arden are also held at Meriden; the most important one, known as the Grand Wardmote, is held in July. The Woodmen wear a distinctive uniform of green hats, buff waistcoats and white breeches; although it is said that Robin Hood competed here, their records only date from 1785.

WEST SUSSEX

Chichester Cathedral Plough Sunday Service occurs on the Sunday nearest January 6th. On the Sunday nearest May 1st, the May Queen is crowned and there is dancing in the streets. More folk dancing can be seen in the Bishop's Palace Gardens on Spring Bank Holiday Monday, and on Christmas Morning there is Morris dancing in the streets.

There is an early start to May Day at **Shoreham** for there is dancing in the streets at 6.30 a.m. and the ceremony of "knocking up" local dignitaries. On the first Saturday of the month Maypole dancing takes place in the square outside St. Mary's church.

At **Tinsley Green** near Crawley every Good Friday the British Individual Marbles Championship is held. About the year 1600 two rivals are supposed to have contested for the hand of a local beauty by a game of marbles. Nowadays it is a highly organised team competition played under strict rules and the two players with the highest scores compete for the individual title.

WEST YORKSHIRE

Three Pole Men, elected by the villagers, supervise the lowering of the Maypole (said to be the tallest in England) at **Barwick-in-Elmet** on Easter Monday every third year for repainting. After its re-erection on Whit Tuesday there is a display of Maypole dancing.

The first **Denby Dale** pie was baked in 1788, and six have been made since then to mark various notable events; the one in 1964 was to celebrate the birth of four Royal babies in one year. The huge pie was cut up and pieces sold for charity.

At **Dewsbury** on Christmas Eve the Devil's Knell is tolled. Beginning at 11 p.m. one stroke is tolled for every year since the birth of Christ—the holy birth heralding the Devil's decease. The May Day celebrations at **Gawthorpe** include all the traditional events—the crowning of the May Queen, a spectacular procession and Morris dancing.

August 5th, which is the feast of St. Oswald, is the date for the annual "Church Clipping" at **Guiseley,** where he is the patron saint of the parish. The Sunday School anniversary at **Haworth** at the end of July is marked by a Rushbearing ceremony.

Schoolboys at **Midgley** perform a traditional Pace Egg Play on Good Friday using a text which dates back to the eighteenth century. This resembles the other Mumming Plays, and includes such characters as St. George, Toss Pot (representing evil), the Doctor and the King of Egypt. Several performances are given in the area throughout the day.

WILTSHIRE

The 200-year old annual dinner for "threshers and labourers", known as the Duck Feast, is held at **Charlton St. Peter** near Upavon, to commemorate the Reverend Stephen Duck who was born here and became known as the Thresher Poet.

The annual Tayler Charity service at **Keevil** church on the Wednesday of Easter week is followed by a distribution of buns. Under the terms of this bequest a "sermon is to be preached suited to the capacity of children and young persons" after which a fourpenny cake must be provided for each teacher present and a twopenny cake for each scholar. In this day and age the cakes provided usually cost more than this!

Malmesbury Old Corporation Courts are held four times a year—at Trinity, on King Athelstan's Feast Day a week afterwards, at Michaelmas and on December 31st. These meetings, held in the Courthouse of St. John, near St. John's Bridge, are superintended by the High Steward or the Warden and attended by the Assistant Burgesses, Landholders and Commoners. A grant of land was made to the people of the town by King Athelstan in 930, and various persons are still entitled to a plot, claims for which must be made at the Court.

The Companions of the Most Ancient Order of Druids keep a midnight vigil on June 21st at **Stonehenge** and hold their Summer Solstice Service as the sun shines directly over the altar stone at dawn; a second service is held at noon. Hundreds of people watch this event.

Wishford near Salisbury maintains two old customs. On Rogation Monday the annual sale of Midsummer Tithes takes place. This is a sale of grazing rights on six and a half acres of church land which is conducted by the Parish Clerk or Churchwarden in the churchyard just before sunset. With the church key in his hand the official walks between the church porch and the gate inviting bids. Bidding continues until the sun sinks below the horizon; as soon as it has disappeared he strikes the gate with the key and the rights go to the last person to bid before this occurs.

In 1603 the Wishford villagers were granted the right to gather wood for all time in Grovely Forest, and they ensure this privilege by marching once a year on May 29th to the Forest to cut wood. They return to the village with large branches, and process through the streets carrying a banner bearing the words *Grovely, Grovely, and all Grovely! Unity is Strength,* and shouting the words "Grovely, Grovely and all Grovely".

INDEX